JUL - 2010

RESPIRATION

SUPER COOL
SCIENCE
EXPERIMENTS:
RESPIRATION

by Tamra B. Orr

CHERRY LAKE PUBLISHING • ANN ARBOR, MICHIGAN

CHERRY
LAKE
Publishing

A NOTE TO PARENTS AND TEACHERS: Please review the instructions for these experiments before your children do them. Be sure to help them with any experiments you do not think they can safely conduct on their own.

A NOTE TO KIDS: Be sure to ask an adult for help with these experiments when you need it. Always put your safety first!

Published in the United States of America by
Cherry Lake Publishing
Ann Arbor, Michigan
www.cherrylakepublishing.com

Content Editor: Robert Wolffe, EdD,
Professor of Teacher Education,
Bradley University, Peoria, Illinois

Book design and illustration: The Design Lab

Photo Credits: Cover and page 1, ©Jose AS Reyes, used under license from Shutterstock, Inc.; page 5, ©archana bhartia, used under license from Shutterstock, Inc.; page 8, ©Gleb Semenjuk, used under license from Shutterstock, Inc.; page 11, ©iStockphoto.com/Mlenny; page 13, ©Purestock/Alamy; page 17, ©MedicalRF.com/Alamy; page 20, ©iStockphoto.com/ksass; page 24, ©Lisa F. Young, used under license from Shutterstock, Inc.

Library of Congress Cataloging-in-Publication Data
Orr, Tamra.
  Super cool science experiments: Respiration / by Tamra Orr.
      p. cm.—(Science explorer)
  Includes bibliographical references and index.
  ISBN-13: 978-1-60279-519-8   ISBN-10: 1-60279-519-3 (lib. bdg.)
  ISBN-13: 978-1-60279-598-3   ISBN-10: 1-60279-598-3 (pbk.)
  1. Respiration—Experiments—Juvenile literature. 2.
Lungs—Physiology—Juvenile literature. I. Title. II. Title: Respiration.
III. Series.
  QP121.O77 2010
  612.2'1—dc22   2009005324

Cherry Lake Publishing would like to acknowledge the work of The Partnership for 21st Century Skills. Please visit www.21stcenturyskills.org for more information.

RESPIRATION

TABLE OF CONTENTS

Breathe Easy!

In, out, in, out . . . Your body does it all day, every day. It doesn't matter where you are, or if you are awake or asleep. You don't even think about it! Can you figure out what it is? Breathing! The complete act of breathing, or respiration, is an important body process. The respiratory system is found in your head and chest. This system makes breathing possible.

If you've ever wondered just how breathing works, you are already on your way to thinking like a scientist. In this book, we'll learn how scientists think. We'll do that by experimenting with respiration. Can you believe that you can do experiments with things you already have at home? We'll see just how fun and exciting science can be as we learn all sorts of new things. You might need to catch your breath by the time we're finished!

Can you feel your chest move up and down as you breathe?

4

First Things First

↶ Playing the flute requires respiration.

Scientists learn by carefully studying how things and people work. For example, scientists who study humans watch how they develop. They see which parts of the body do what jobs and how each part is connected. They study the process of breathing and how the respiratory system works. They do experiments to see how the lungs use oxygen and carbon dioxide to keep everything healthy and working like it should.

Good scientists take notes on everything they discover. They write down their observations. Sometimes those observations lead scientists to ask new questions. With new questions in mind, they design experiments to find the answers.

When scientists design experiments, they must think very clearly. The way they think about problems is often called the scientific method. What is the scientific method? It's a step-by-step way of finding answers to specific questions. The steps don't always follow the same pattern. Sometimes scientists change their minds. The process often works something like this:

Scientific method

- **Step One:** A scientist gathers the facts and makes observations about one particular thing.
- **Step Two:** The scientist comes up with a question that is not answered by all the observations and facts.
- **Step Three:** The scientist creates a hypothesis. This is a statement of what the scientist thinks is probably the answer to the question.
- **Step Four:** The scientist tests the hypothesis. He or she designs an experiment to see whether the hypothesis is correct. The scientist does the experiment and writes down what happens.

- **Step Five:** The scientist draws a conclusion based on how the experiment turned out. The conclusion might be that the hypothesis is correct. Sometimes, though, the hypothesis is not correct. In that case, the scientist might develop a new hypothesis and another experiment.

  In the following experiments, we'll see the scientific method in action. We'll gather some facts and observations about respiration. And for each experiment, we'll develop a question and a hypothesis. Next, we'll do an actual experiment to see if our hypothesis is correct. By the end of the experiment, we should know something new about respiration. Scientists, are you ready? Then let's get started!

Don't forget to write down your observations.

Experiment #1
In through
the Nose . . . .

← How important is your nose?

Have you ever thought about how smart your body truly is? Without any effort on your part, it keeps doing countless important jobs. It doesn't matter if you're studying for a test or taking a nap. Your organs and body systems still do what they need to do. Your heart keeps beating. Your eyes keep blinking. Your lungs keep breathing. It's a good thing, too. If any of these processes stopped, you would quickly be in big trouble.

Each day, you breathe about 20,000 times. How important is breathing? It is easy to find out. Take a deep breath and hold it. Watch the clock. Isn't it amazing how long a minute can be? How about 2 minutes? If you're like most people, you will soon start to struggle and need to take a breath.

Respiration starts with your mouth and nose. Most of the time, you breathe in through your nose. If you've ever had a cold, you know that you can also breathe through your mouth. When you exercise and need bigger quantities of oxygen, you tend to breathe through your mouth also.

For our first hypothesis, let's ask ourselves some interesting questions about breathing. For example, how do our nostrils work when we breathe? Do both of our nostrils take in and breathe out the same amount of air? Think about it. Come up with a hypothesis. Here is one option: **The same amount of air passes through each nostril.**

Here's what you'll need:
- A small hand or pocket mirror
- Paper
- A pencil

There aren't many items needed for this experiment.

Instructions:

1. First, blow out or exhale through your nostrils onto your hand. Can you feel the warmth? As air travels through your body, it picks up heat.

2. Now hold the mirror up to your nose. Put it below your nose but above your upper lip. Keep it horizontal.

3. Breathe gently out of your nose onto the mirror.

4. Look at the mirror. Do you see condensation? It looks like fog clouding up the mirror.

5. Look carefully. Can you see two spots, one from each nostril? The moisture from the breath of each nostril created condensation. Is one area of condensation bigger than the other? What does that suggest about the amount of air that passed through each nostril? Was your hypothesis correct?

Conclusion:

Believe it or not, each nostril takes turns being the one through which most of your breath passes. Write down the time and which side seems to be doing the most work at this time. Then wait 2 or 3 hours and repeat the experiment. You will likely see that most air now passes through the opposite nostril.

How long can you hold your breath?

On April 30, 2008, magician and daredevil David Blaine set a new world record for holding his breath: 17 minutes and 4.4 seconds. How was this possible? It required weeks and weeks of practicing and training. Blaine also learned the art of lung packing. Lung packing is the practice of forcing large amounts of air into the lungs.

Experiment #2
Down the Windpipe

Breathing is all about inhaling, or breathing in, and then exhaling, or letting the breath out. When we take breath in, we are using the oxygen in the air. We need it for every cell in our bodies to grow and function. After we use up the oxygen, however, we are left with a gas we don't need: carbon dioxide. It is considered a waste gas. Respiration is all about exchanging these gases. Too much of either gas would be bad news for us! Let's see how this process works.

Once you take in a breath, what happens? First, the air passes through the trachea, or windpipe. This is the tube that connects your mouth and nose to your lungs. The trachea is about 4 inches (10.2 centimeters) long and less than 1 inch (2.5 cm) around. It is made up of 20 C-shaped pieces of strong, bendy tissue called cartilage. This cartilage helps keep the trachea from collapsing. If you reach up and carefully feel the front of your throat, you can detect the parts that make up the trachea.

The inside of your trachea is covered in tiny hairs called cilia. As you breathe, they gently move back and forth, keeping mucus, dust, and dirt from getting into your lungs. Much of this junk is coughed out. If it goes up toward your nose, however, you might have to sneeze. Sneezes are incredibly powerful. They send particles flying out of your nose at an amazing 100 miles per hour (161 kilometers per hour).

Inhaling brings oxygen into your body. After your cells use that oxygen, they produce carbon dioxide. How does carbon dioxide leave your body? Could it be through exhaling? That question is a good focus for our next experiment. Come up with a hypothesis. Or test this one: **When we breathe out,**

If you could see inside your neck, you'd see your trachea.

we exhale carbon dioxide. Let's find the answer by doing an experiment.

Here's what you'll need:

- An adult helper
- Red cabbage
- A sharp knife
- A pot (not aluminum)
- Water
- A strainer
- A clear glass
- A straw

Have an adult help chop the cabbage.

Instructions:

1. With an adult's help, chop up some red cabbage.
2. Put the cabbage into a pot, and cover it with water.
3. Heat the cabbage on the stove until it begins to boil. It should keep boiling until the water turns purple.

What happens when you blow into the liquid?

4. Take the cabbage off the heat. Let the water and cabbage mixture cool.
5. Use the strainer to pour the juices from the pot into a clear glass. Do not fill the glass all the way to the top.
6. Put a straw in the glass and blow into it. Watch carefully.

Conclusion:

What happens to the color of the juice as you blow into the straw? Slowly, it will change from purple to pink. This is because carbon dioxide is an acid. When it mixes with the juice, the color changes. What does this fact tell you about the air you exhale? Does it contain carbon dioxide? Based on your observations, you can conclude that it does. Your hypothesis was correct!

Experiment #3
A Trip through the Bronchi

At the bottom of your trachea are two large tubes. They are called the bronchi. One connects to the left lung, while the other connects to the right one. By itself, each tube is called a bronchus. Inside your lungs, the bronchi branch out like the limbs on a tree. As they spread out, they get smaller and smaller. The tiniest ones are about as thick as a strand of hair. These are called bronchioles. Each lung has about 30,000 of them!

If that sounds like a lot, wait until you hear what's next. At the end of each and every one of those tiny bronchioles are bunches of even tinier air sacs known as alveoli. You have about 600 *million*

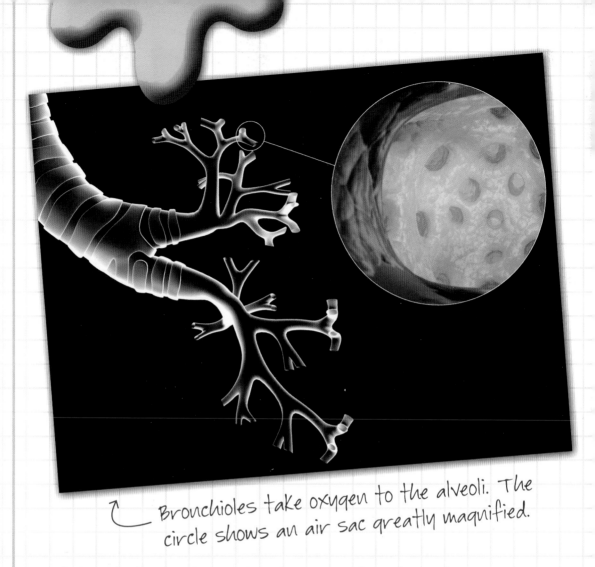

Bronchioles take oxygen to the alveoli. The circle shows an air sac greatly magnified.

of them! Think of the alveoli as tiny bunches of grapes at the end of the bronchioles. As small as alveoli are, there are so many that if you could stretch them out flat, they would cover a whole tennis court.

Can you guess what happens to your lungs when you inhale and air reaches all of these alveoli? Let's test a new hypothesis: **When alveoli fill up with air, the chest has to expand to make room.** Is it true? Let's find out.

Here's what you'll need:

- A clear 16- to 20-ounce (about ½ liter) plastic bottle
- Water
- Food coloring
- A straw
- A small lump of clay

Gather your supplies before you begin.

Instructions:

1. Start by filling the bottle halfway with water. Then add a few drops of food coloring.
2. Next, put the straw in the bottle, and place the clay over the bottle's opening. This should hold the straw in place, so it does not come out of the bottle. The straw is like your trachea, while the clay is like your throat. The bottle is your chest. The movement of the water represents the movement of air in and out of your lungs.
3. Now push in on the bottle with your hand.
4. Watch what happens to the bottle. Do you see

Squeeze the bottle with one hand.

NOTES

how it gets smaller? It is because the water has been pushed out. When you stop pushing on the bottle, it gets bigger. This is from air pressure pushing the water back in.

Conclusion:

How did this experiment show you how your chest changes as you breathe in and out? Take a few extra breaths now. Can you picture the air sacs filling up and then emptying? That is what respiration is all about.

Experiment #4
What a Pair of
Lungs

Lungs take up a lot of room in your chest.

Have you ever noticed how your body seems to have so many sets of 2? You have 2 eyes, 2 ears, 2 arms, and 2 legs. You also have 2 lungs. Compared to some of the other organs in your body, the lungs are pretty big. They take up most of the room in your chest. The one on the left is slightly smaller than the one on the right because it has to make room for your heart. Because your heart and lungs are so vital to living, they are protected by 12 pairs of rib bones connected to your sternum, or breastbone.

When you imagine what your lungs are like, you may picture them as large, hollow bags or balloons. They are actually much more like pink, squishy sponges. As you've already learned, they are not empty either. They are full of bronchioles and alveoli.

They expand when you breathe in and contract when you breathe out.

How much air can a set of lungs hold? Do you think your body's size affects how much air your lungs can hold? Think about the second question. Come up with a hypothesis. Here are three options to choose from:

Hypothesis #1: A smaller person's lungs hold less air than a larger person's lungs.

Hypothesis #2: A smaller person's lungs hold the same amount of air as a larger person's lungs.

Hypothesis #3: A smaller person's lungs hold more air than a larger person's lungs.

Here's what you'll need:
- A large dishpan or sink
- Water
- An empty 1-gallon (3.8 liter) milk bottle with a lid
- A funnel
- 2 flexible drinking straws
- An adult helper

Choose an adult helper who is bigger than you are.

Instructions:

1. Fill a dishpan or sink with 2 inches (5 cm) of water.
2. Fill the milk bottle all the way to the top with water. You may need to pour the water through the funnel to keep it from spilling. Put the lid on tightly. Most likely, a little water will squirt out when you do.
3. Now, holding the lid, turn the bottle upside down. Place the mouth of the bottle under the water in the dishpan.
4. Carefully reach under the water and unscrew the lid. Set the lid to the side.

Be careful! You don't want to have to clean up a watery mess!

5. Bend the straw and put the shorter end into the mouth of the bottle under the water. The longer end should stick up out of the water.
6. Have an adult hold the bottle while you hold the straw.
7. Pinch your nose closed and take a deep breath.
8. Blow all of your air into the straw in one strong breath. What happens to the water in the bottle?
9. Now reach in and put the lid back on the bottle tightly.
10. Remove the bottle from the dishpan. Set it on the table. How much water is in the bottle now?
11. Repeat the experiment. This time, have an adult blow into the second straw. What happens to the water in the bottle this time?

Conclusion:

When you breathed into the straw, some water was forced out of the bottle. The amount of empty space you created in the bottle represents the amount of air that was in your lungs. How do your results compare to an adult's? Did the adult force more water out of the bottle? If so, why do you think that is? Most adults have bigger bodies than children. Their lungs are larger, too. And larger lungs can hold more air. Does this help explain your results? Was your hypothesis correct?

Experiment #5
It Takes
Muscles

A singer must learn to control her breath with her diaphragm.

With all of the movement your chest and lungs do, you might think that they have strong muscles. The surprise is that your lungs do not have any muscles in them at all. Instead, a nearby muscle called the diaphragm plays a big role in helping them do their job.

The diaphragm is a dome-shaped muscle beneath your lungs. As you take a breath, the muscle flattens out and moves lower. This creates more space in your chest for your lungs, which get bigger when they fill with air. When the space in the chest is increased, it lowers the pressure in the lungs. So air moves into the lungs, and they get bigger to fill the space. The muscles surrounding your ribs also help make space. These muscles lift the ribs up and out, so your lungs can fill up.

What do you think happens to the diaphragm when you exhale? Come up with a hypothesis that focuses on the diaphragm. Here is one option: **As you exhale, the diaphragm relaxes and moves up.**

Here's what you'll need:
- Scissors
- 1 straw
- 2 small balloons
- 2 small rubber bands
- Rubber cement
- Tape
- 1 clear plastic cup
- 1 large balloon
- 1 large rubber band

You can buy rubber cement at a craft or office supply store.

Instructions:

1. Cut two 2-inch (5 cm) pieces of straw from the straw. Cut a small triangle in the center of one of the 2-inch pieces. Do not cut through the opposite side of the straw.

2. Fit 1 small balloon over each end of the 2-inch piece of straw, securing each balloon with a small rubber band.

3. Bend the straw in the middle of the triangular hole.

4. Next, take the second 2-inch piece of straw and gently hold one end closed. Cut a V shape at one end of the straw. Make sure you cut through both sides of the straw so that you have two slanted points at one end of the piece of straw.

5. Fit the slanted points into the openings on each side of the bent straw. Using the rubber cement, glue the two pieces of the straw together. Put tape over the seal you made with the rubber cement, and give it at least 30 minutes to dry.

6. While it is drying, cut a hole

Use rubber cement to glue the straws together.

in the bottom of the clear plastic cup. Make the hole the same width as the straw. Push the second 2-inch piece of straw through the hole in the bottom of the cup so that the small balloons and the straw they are attached to are now inside the plastic cup. Use the rubber cement to glue the second 2-inch piece of straw into the hole.

7. Next, take the large balloon and cut the neck off of it. Stretch it carefully over the opening of the cup. Don't crack the cup. Secure the edges with the large rubber band.

8. Pull the large balloon gently. Observe what happens to the small balloons. Let go of the large balloon. What happens to the small balloons now?

Conclusion:

The large balloon represents your diaphragm. Pulling the large balloon re-creates what happens when you inhale. When you pulled the balloon, you created more space in the cup and the pressure decreased. So air entered the small lung balloons. What happened when you released the large balloon? Did it move back into its original position? What happened to the lung balloons? Releasing the large balloon re-creates what happens when you exhale. Your diaphragm and rib muscles have relaxed. With less space in the chest, the pressure increases. The air is forced out of your lungs. Did you prove your hypothesis?

Experiment #6

Do It Yourself!

Now you know many things about respiration and your respiratory system. You learned through your observations and experiments. You even created hypotheses and tested them! So what's next?

How about coming up with your own experiment? First, you need to think of a question that you would like to answer. For example, have you ever wondered how many breaths you take in a minute? Do you think different activities might change the number of breaths you take each minute? What kinds of activities might affect your breathing the most? Come up with answers to these questions. Then test them!

Think about the materials you will need to test this experiment. Write out a list of these materials. Then write out the instructions for your experiment. Work with a friend, a classmate, or a family member to perform your experiment, and record your results. Congratulations! You're now a full-fledged scientist.

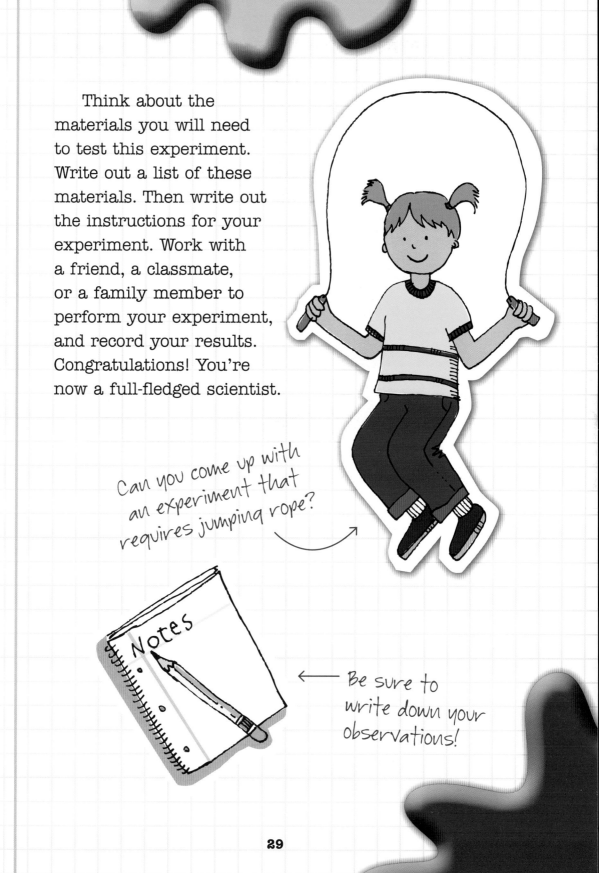

Can you come up with an experiment that requires jumping rope?

Notes

← Be sure to write down your observations!

GLOSSARY

alveoli (al-VEE-uh-lye) tiny, air-filled sacs in the lungs

bronchioles (BRONG-kee-olz) tiny extensions of the bronchi

bronchus (BRONG-kus) one branch of the trachea

carbon dioxide (KAR-buhn dye-OK-side) a gas that is a mixture of carbon and oxygen

cartilage (KAR-til-ij) an elastic type of connective tissue

conclusion (kuhn-KLOO-zhuhn) a final decision, thought, or opinion

hypothesis (hy-POTH-uh-sihss) a logical guess about what will happen in an experiment

method (METH-uhd) a way of doing something

observations (ob-zur-VAY-shuhnz) things that are seen or noticed with one's senses

respiration (res-puh-REY-shuhn) the inhalation and exhalation of air

trachea (TREY-kee-uh) the windpipe that connects the mouth to the lungs

FOR MORE INFORMATION

BOOKS

Ballard, Carol. *The Lungs and Breathing.* Detroit: KidHaven Press, 2005.

Simon, Seymour. *Lungs: Your Respiratory System.* New York: Collins, 2007.

Spilsbury, Louise. *Respiration and Circulation.* Chicago: Heinemann, 2008.

WEB SITES

Discovery Kids—Your Respiratory System
yucky.discovery.com/flash/body/pg000138.html
Find fun facts about breathing and the respiratory system

KidsHealth—Your Lungs & Respiratory System
kidshealth.org/kid/cancer_center/HTBW/lungs.html
For more information about lungs and breathing

Saskatchewan Lung Association—Inside the Human Body: The Respiratory System
lung.ca/children/index_kids.html
Fun stories and games about the human body

INDEX

About the →
Author

Tamra Orr is the author of more than 200 nonfiction books for readers of all ages. She loves doing research. Orr lives in the Pacific Northwest with her husband, three teenagers, a cat, and a dog. She has a teaching degree from Ball State University and in her few minutes of spare time, she likes to write old-fashioned letters, read books, and look at the snowcapped mountains.